For Reference

Not to be taken from this room

Cotton

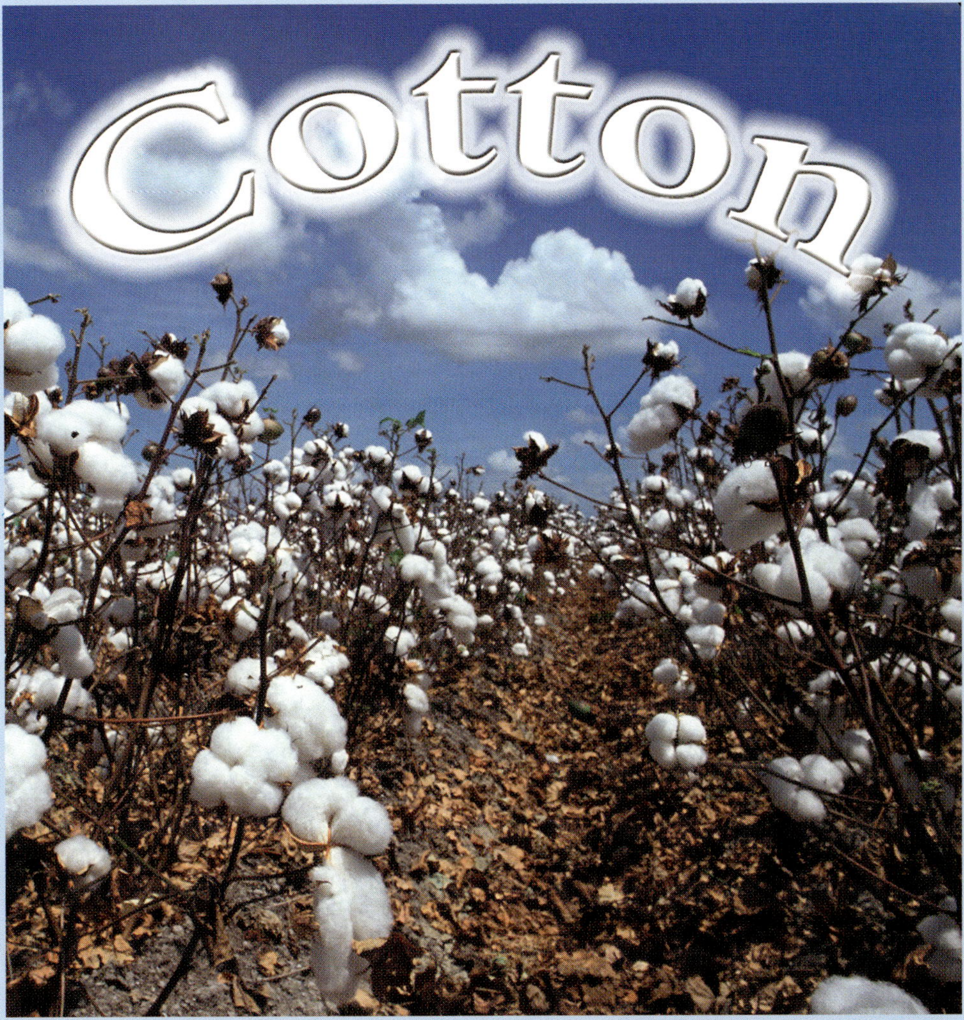

Irene Franck and David Brownstone

GROLIER

An imprint of Scholastic Library Publishing
Danbury, Connecticut

Credits and Acknowledgments

abbreviations: t (top), b (bottom), l (left), r (right), c (center)
Image credits: Agricultural Research Service Library: 1b and 19 (David Nance); 9l, 20, 21 and 25 (Scott Bauer); Art Resource: 17 (Victoria and Albert Museum), 22 (New York Public Library/Spencer Collection, The New York Public Library Astor, Lenox, and Tilden Foundations), 27 (Newark Museum); Getty Images: 29l (Stone/Willie Maldonado); Getty Images/PhotoDisc: 26 (Ryan McVay); Getty Images/PhotoDisc/PhotoLink: 6l and 6r (S. Solum); 3, 4, 10, 11, 13b; Library of Congress: 16t; National Aeronautics and Space Administration (NASA): 1t and running heads; North Wind Pictures: 18; Photo Researchers, Inc.: 5 (Jim Steinberg), 7 (George Bolton), 8l (R. E. Litchfield/Science Photo Library), 9r (Harry Rogers), 14 (Lee Snyder), 15 (Wesley Bocxe), 23 (Aaron Haupt), 28 (Carl Frank), 29r (Science Photo Library); U.S. Department of Agriculture: 24 (Ken Hammond); Woodfin Camp & Associates: 8r (Mike Yamashita), 16b (Lindsay Hebberd); World Bank: 12 (Ray Witlin). Original image created for this book by K & P Publishing Services: 13t.

Our thanks to Joe Hollander, Phil Friedman, and Laurie McCurley at Scholastic Library Publishing; to photo researchers Susan Hormuth, Robin Sand, and Robert Melcak; to copy editor Michael Burke; and to the librarians throughout the northeastern library network, in particular to the staff of the Chappaqua Library—director Mark Hasskarl; the expert reference staff, including Martha Alcott, Michele J. Capozzella, Maryanne Eaton, Catherine Paulsen, Jane Peyraud, Paula Peyraud, and Carolyn Reznick; and the circulation staff, headed by Barbara Le Sauvage—for fulfilling our wide-ranging research needs.

Published 2003 by Grolier
Division of Scholastic Library Publishing
Old Sherman Turnpike
Danbury, Connecticut 06816

For information address the publisher:
Scholastic Library Publishing, Grolier Division
Old Sherman Turnpike, Danbury, Connecticut 06816

© 2003 Irene M. Franck and David M. Brownstone

All rights reserved. Except for use in a review, no part of this book may be reproduced, stored in a retrieval system, or transmitted in any form, or by any means, electronic or mechanical, including photocopying, recording, or otherwise, without prior permission of Scholastic Library Publishing.

Library of Congress Cataloging-in-Publication Data

Franck, Irene M.
    Cotton / Irene Franck and David Brownstone.
      p. cm. -- (Riches of the earth ; v. 2)
    Summary: Provides information about cotton and its importance in everyday life.
    Includes bibliographical references and index.
    ISBN 0-7172-5730-4 (set : alk. paper) -- ISBN 0-7172-5714-2 (vol. 2 : alk paper)
    1. Cotton--Juvenile literature [1. Cotton.] I. Brownstone, David M. II. Title.

TS1576.F73 2003
677'.21--dc21

2003044078

Printed in the United States of America

Designed by K & P Publishing Services

Contents

Cotton Yesterday and Today 4

What Is Cotton? 6

    Sweet Cellulose 8

Cotton around the World 12

Cotton in History 14

From Field to Mill 19

Cotton into Yarn 22

Yarn into Cloth 27

Words to Know 30

On the Internet 31

In Print 31

Index 32

T-shirts, sweatshirts, and jeans—like those worn by these young people fishing—have traditionally been made of all cotton. That remains so today, though some are now made of cotton mixed with other fabrics.

Cotton Yesterday and Today

We all use cotton, and probably in more ways than we know. We wear shirts, pants, dresses, underwear, socks, raincoats, and all kinds of other clothes made of cotton. We sleep on sheets, pillowcases, and mattresses made of cotton, dry ourselves with towels and robes made of cotton, sit on chairs covered with and stuffed with cotton, and blow our noses in handkerchiefs made of cotton. We even eat cotton, in the form of shortening (a fat used in cooking) made out of cottonseed oil.

In short, cotton is one of the most basic substances in our lives. That has been so for many thousands of years. Highly skilled spinners and

Cotton Yesterday and Today

One of the reasons for cotton's popularity is that it can be dyed so many bright and beautiful colors, like the threads and yarns shown here.

weavers in all the great ancient civilizations—from China, India, and Egypt in the Old World to Mexico and Peru in the Americas—created clothing and many other kinds of cotton goods for everyone from commoners to kings.

In the modern world we have found far more uses for cotton than ever before. We also grow and consume a great deal more cotton than people in the ancient world did. Every year cotton growers in many countries—most of all in the United States—reap a huge harvest that yields billions of pounds of cotton from hundreds of millions of cotton plants.

During the past century humans have invented many fabrics that are synthetic (not grown naturally). Even so, cotton is still the world's most widely used clothing material. There are now at least 6 billion people on Earth, compared with 2 billion a century ago. That means vastly increased demand for cotton to meet the needs of the world's fast-growing population.

Not so long ago cotton was picked, processed, spun, and woven by hand, in quantities that were tiny by today's standards. Today all that is done by machine, in huge quantities by any standard.

Here then is the story of cotton, as it was yesterday but mostly as it is today.

This is a cotton flower as it is just beginning to bloom, in the early stages of the life of a cotton plant. Later the petals drop off and the *boll* (seed pod) forms, in which cotton grows.

This is a fully ripe cotton boll (right), bursting open and showing the white cotton fibers inside. At the top is another cotton boll, which is not yet ripe but still growing.

What Is Cotton?

Cotton is a soft, usually creamy-white kind of fiber (a threadlike material that can be spun into yarn). It grows as thin, strong hairs out of the seeds of the cotton plant.

Cotton fibers are much longer than they are thick. A single seed of the most common kind of cotton used in clothing grows 10,000 to 20,000 fibers. Each of these fibers is only a few *millionths* of a meter thick (a meter is a little under 40 inches).

Cotton fibers naturally twist together to form longer *slivers* of cotton. After processing, these slivers can be spun together into long strands of yarn that can later be made into cloth.

Colorfully dyed cotton threads are used in weaving and also in stitching designs into cloth. This modern cotton cloth from Panama has a striking added design (appliqués) showing a helicopter and its passengers.

Although most cotton is white, some kinds of cottons are naturally of other colors. Several very high-quality Egyptian Giza cottons are light brown, and American-grown Pima cotton is a brown-tinted white. These Egyptian and American cottons are used to make high-quality thread and cloth. Green, red, and several other kinds of naturally colored cottons have also long been grown.

Most colored cottons are dyed, using dyes and dyeing processes that often go back thousands of years. However, we now know that many dyes are very harmful to the environment. Because of that, the late 20th century and the early 21st century have seen more development of naturally colored cottons.

Cotton is largely (about 90 percent) made of *cellulose*, an important part of the structure of all plants (see p. 8). Beyond that, cotton contains some water and several other substances found in all plants.

Cotton

Sweet Cellulose

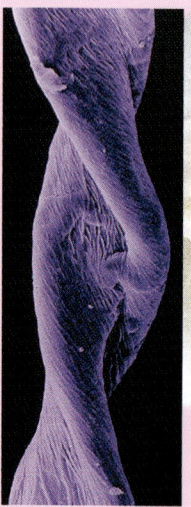

Cellulose is found in all plants. It is a *carbohydrate*, a kind of chemical *compound* (mixed material) made of just three *elements* (basic materials): carbon, hydrogen, and oxygen.

Carbon, hydrogen, and oxygen can form many compounds. In cellulose they form themselves into units of *glucose*. Glucose is the main kind of sugar that many living beings—including humans—use as their basic source of energy. So cotton is made mostly of sugar!

Humans don't find cotton good for eating. But some insects do, such as the *boll weevil*, which can attack the cotton plant and spoil the crop.

This is what a single cotton fiber looks like, when magnified 400 times. (The enlarging machine gave the white cotton fiber a false color.)

Varieties of Cotton

There are more than 30 varieties of cotton plants, growing in many parts of the world. (All are part of a group of plants known to biologists as *Gossypium*.) Most grow in the wild. Only a few are cultivated (grown deliberately by farmers). Some kinds of cotton plants grow as high as 20 feet. However, the kinds that are most often cultivated grow three to four feet high.

Cotton grows within the *boll* (seed pod) at the center of a cotton flower. As the flower goes through its own growth cycle, the petals dry up and drop off, and the boll becomes larger and more packed with cotton fibers. Several months after the plant has started to flower, and after the petals have dropped away, the cotton-packed boll pops open, releasing the cotton inside. It is then ready to be picked.

Three kinds of tremendously useful substances come out of the plant's seeds. Two of them are kinds of cotton fibers, and the third is the seed itself. First—and by far the most important of the three—is *lint*. This is the main body of the cotton fibers harvested from the cotton

 *What Is Cotton?*

One of the cotton farmer's worst enemies is the boll weevil, shown here (left) on the outside of a cotton boll (with a pink petal showing in the background). It eats into the boll and damages or destroys the cotton inside.

This young, unripened cotton boll has been cut open to show the damage caused inside by the larva (wormlike form) of the boll weevil.

plant. Lint fibers grow in several lengths, depending on the variety of cotton plants. Lint fibers range from half an inch to two inches long. The longer fibers yield the best quality cotton.

Long-staple varieties are at least $1^{1}/_{8}$ inches long. *Medium-staple* varieties are $1^{1}/_{32}$ inches to $1^{3}/_{32}$ inches long. *Short-staple* varieties are less than an inch long.

By far the most widely used of the American cottons are the several American Upland varieties, which make up 97 percent of the American cotton crop. Upland cotton fibers are $^{7}/_{8}$ inch to $1^{1}/_{4}$ inches long.

Several very high quality cottons

9

Cotton

are the Sea Island, Egyptian, and American Pima varieties, some of them up to $1 5/8$ inches long. Asiatic cotton, grown largely in Asia, is of poorer quality than the longer-staple cottons and has fibers less than an inch long.

The second of the highly useful substances from the seed is the very short fiber called the *linter* or *fuzz*. From $1/8$ to $1/4$ inch long, linter is left over on the cottonseeds after the seeds have been separated from the cotton in the ginning process (see p. 19). Cotton linters are used in several products (see p. 20).

The third of the substances is the seed itself. This is ultimately used in a wide range of products (see p. 20).

Qualities of Cotton

Cotton has many advantages. It absorbs water and other liquids very easily. That makes it ideal for towels, robes, diapers, handkerchiefs, and many kinds of sports-

Many athletes have long preferred cotton because it absorbs moisture and is strong and longlasting. T-shirts like those worn by these rugby players are traditionally made of cotton.

What Is Cotton?

This cotton boll has been turned into a Christmas ornament by the addition of gold wings and halo.

wear. Heat also flows easily through it, so cotton clothing is cool in hot weather.

Cotton also isn't harmed by extremely high temperatures. That means cotton sheets, towels, and other items can be boiled to kill germs, making them safe to use in homes and hospitals.

Cotton yarns are tight, rather than loose, so they can be made into very closely woven fabrics, not just clothes but also textiles for other kinds of uses. The canvas used to make sails for a boat or a painting surface for an artist, for example, is often made of cotton. Cotton is also widely used in draperies and carpets, sometimes interwoven with other kinds of yarns, such as wool, silk, or artificial fibers.

Cotton can be dyed a whole range of bright and beautiful colors. It may be dyed as threads or as woven fabric. And the fabric may be dyed one color or a variety of colors, as by a hand painter or a printing machine. Over time, the dyes fade somewhat, as in an old pair of jeans. That is why draperies are often lined to protect them from the sunlight.

Cotton also has some disadvantages. Natural cotton wrinkles easily and requires ironing to smooth out the wrinkles. Cotton also burns. Today clothing made of cotton is often treated to make it resistant to both burning and wrinkling.

Cotton can be damaged by some insects and, when damp, may get discolored and smelly from mildew (a fungus). However, it is not damaged by moths, as wool is.

Cotton's advantages are many and clearly outweigh its disadvantages. It is no wonder that cotton is by far the most widely worn and used fabric in the world.

11

The face of this young West African boy is in the shadow of the full basket of cotton picked in the field where he works.

Cotton around the World

Cotton is grown all over the world, but only in warm climates. That is because it has a growing season that lasts seven months or more, and it must have at least six months without frost, which can damage the cotton plant. Cotton needs water, but not too much at harvesting time. Heavy rain when cotton is ready for picking can badly damage the cotton crop.

Where Cotton Is Grown

More than 40 countries produce substantial quantities of cotton. The United States is the world's leading cotton producer. Other major cotton-producing countries include China, India, Pakistan, Russia, and Brazil. In the ancient world India and China were also great cotton-producing countries, as were Egypt, Peru, and Mexico. All still produce cotton.

Cotton around the World

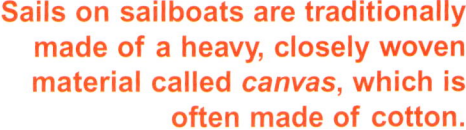

Main cotton-growing and cotton-working regions, past and present

In the United States cotton is grown in a broad sweep of states with warm climates that runs from the Atlantic to the Pacific. About one-third of American cotton is grown in Texas, and substantial amounts are also grown in California, Mississippi, Arkansas, Alabama, Arizona, Tennessee, and Georgia.

Sails on sailboats are traditionally made of a heavy, closely woven material called *canvas*, which is often made of cotton.

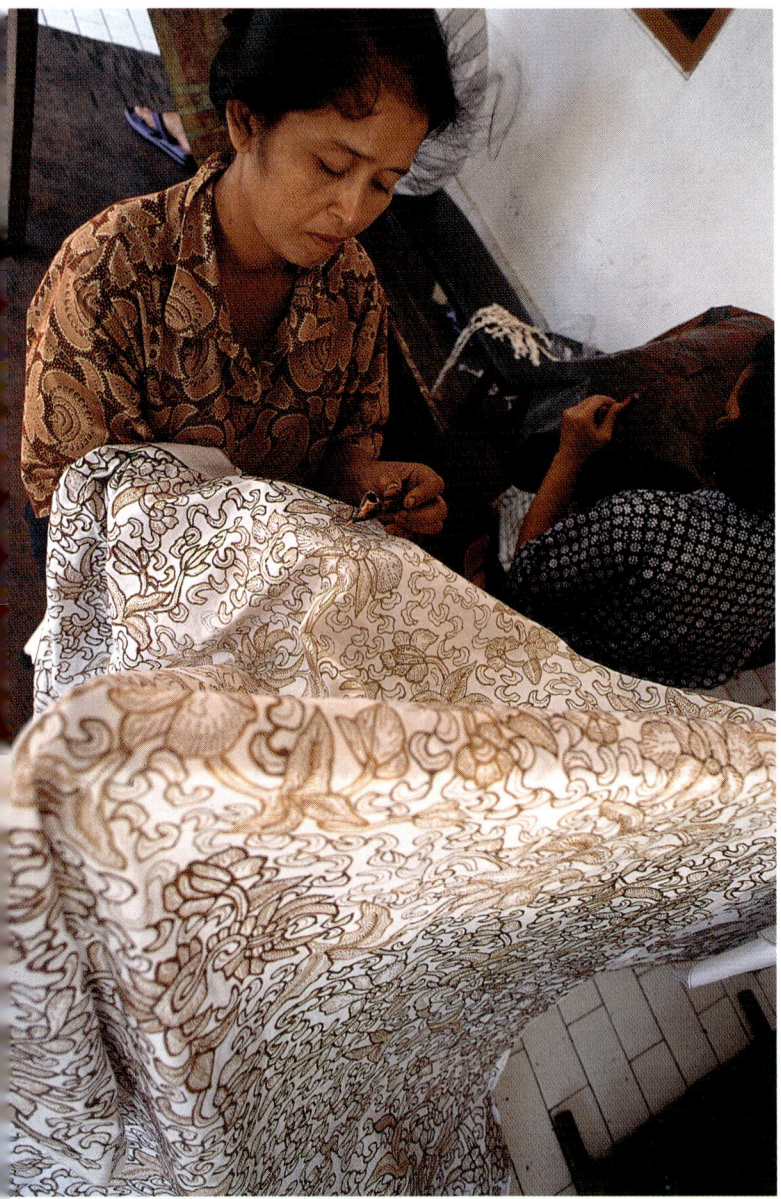

This woman from Bali, an island in Indonesia, is using an age-old technique to decorate cotton fabric. Using the batik method, she is painting a design on the fabric in wax. The fabric is dyed and then the wax is removed, leaving the pattern in the undyed portion of the fabric.

Cotton in History

Cotton has had an important place in human history for at least 7,000 years. It has also played a special role in world history and American history, starting a little before the American nation was born.

Cotton and other fabrics have far shorter lives than most other objects from ancient times found by archaeologists. Because of that, it is very hard to know when people began to use cotton for clothing or for any of its many other purposes. Remnants (pieces) of cotton found in Turkey have been dated as far back as 7,000 years ago (5000 B.C.). However, even earlier cotton remnants may be found as archaeologists discover more about the history of humanity.

Clearly cotton was widely used in

Cotton in History

the ancient world. The early civilizations of central Mexico, Guatemala, and Peru knew and used cotton, some as long as 7,000 years ago and possibly even earlier. At least 3,000 years ago Native Americans in Ecuador and Peru were making large quantities of high-quality cotton clothing, along with some of the world's finest woven cotton artworks.

India's great Indus Valley civilization was using cotton thread and possibly also cotton cloth 3,500 to 4,000 years ago. Somewhat later, but still thousands of years ago, Egypt began to produce clothing and other goods of cotton. These were made of the long-staple, very high quality cotton that today is still some of the best cotton grown anywhere in the world. By 3,000 years ago cotton was being used for many purposes in Babylonia, Assyria, Greece, Rome, and throughout the Middle East and Mediterranean worlds. It continued to be a widely used fabric for clothing and

Traditional ways of making cotton fabrics survive in some parts of the world. In Guatemala many women continue to weave traditional brightly colored cotton fabrics, like those shown for sale here.

15

Cotton

Developed in the United States, the cotton gin soon spread around the world. Dating from about 1898, this image shows a cotton gin in the region of Dahomey (in what is now Benin) in West Africa.

The main obstacle to large-scale cotton production was the seeds, like the ones shown here against a background of cotton. Before the invention of the cotton gin, the seeds had to be picked out by hand, a tiresome job.

other purposes through the Middle Ages and the Renaissance, right up through modern times.

The Factory System

Cotton has played an unusual role in world history. During the 1700s a series of new industrial machines were invented, most of them in Britain. In the same period a new way of mass-producing goods was invented, helped by the new machines. The total result was the development of the *factory system* of mass-producing goods. This system allowed goods to be produced faster and cheaper than by the older methods of production, in which pieces were made by hand, one by one.

The factory system was first applied to cotton products. The new ways of producing cotton then became models for producing all of the main products of the industrial world, including Europe and the United States.

Throughout history, cotton fibers had been slowly separated from cottonseeds by hand. However, the new and cheaper ways of producing cotton goods created much more demand for cotton than could be met by the old methods. That problem was solved by Eli Whitney's invention of the *cotton gin* in 1793. This invention for the first time made it possible to separate cotton fibers from the seeds by machine, many times faster than could be done by hand.

Cotton and Slavery

The factory system and the cotton gin together had enormous impact on cotton production, especially in the American South. This quickly became by far the world's leading cotton-producing area. It also had a very special effect on the history of slavery in the United States and on the coming of the Civil War.

With much greater and cheaper supplies of cotton available, and

The modern factory system was first developed in England in the cotton industry, making that country a center for cotton manufacturing. This is a dress of fancy printed cotton dating from the late 1820s, today preserved in London's Victoria and Albert Museum.

much faster and cheaper ways of turning cotton into finished goods, Britain became the world's leading producer of cotton products. It also began to become the world's great-

Cotton

Though slavery had already been ended in some other countries by the mid-1800s, in the American South large numbers of slaves were forced to work in the cotton fields. That ended only with the Civil War.

est and wealthiest industrial power. At the same time the American South became Britain's main cotton supplier.

Southern cotton growers had developed a slave-based *plantation* system. Slavery had long been established in the American South. However, in the late 1700s it seemed to be on its way out in the United States and elsewhere, for many people in the North and throughout the world saw slavery as antihuman.

However, with the development of the cotton gin, cotton growers depended more and more on the slave-based plantation system for their income. They saw that system as vitally important.

Eventually, under great pressure to end slavery and fearful of a future without it, the South tried to secede (withdraw) from the United States. The North refused to let that happen, and in 1861 the Civil War began.

Most cotton today is picked by machines like this one. They sweep through the fields, cutting off the cotton plants and starting the long process of separating the bolls from the rest of the plant.

From Field to Mill

The cotton gin solved the problem of how to separate cotton fibers from cottonseeds by machine (see p. 17). However, cotton ready for harvesting still had to be picked by hand. That would remain so until the 1950s, when mechanical cotton pickers were invented. Much of the world's cotton is now picked far less expensively by machine. However, even today, cotton in some countries is still picked by hand.

The picked cotton contains seeds, their attached fibers (*lint* and *linters*; see p. 8), and *waste* (*trash*). After harvesting, the cotton is taken to one of the world's tens of thousands of cotton gins. These are all

Cotton

The unginned cotton on the left contains a lot of "trash," including twigs, bits of leaves, and seeds. These get taken out during the ginning process, leaving the cotton clean, white, and ready for processing, like that on the right.

built on the same principle as Eli Whitney's early cotton gin.

The first step in ginning cotton is to separate out and throw away the trash. Then the remaining cotton is run through the gin. This machine pulls the longer cotton fibers (lint) through its narrow, saw-toothed separator and cuts the lint away from the seeds, which cannot fit through. The much shorter cotton fibers (linters) are left behind, still attached to the seeds.

The longer cotton fibers, now cut loose, are then machine-pressed into 500-pound bales. Then the bales move on to warehouses or directly to cotton mills. There the process of turning raw cotton into cloth and other cotton products continues (see p. 22).

Seeds and Linters

The cottonseeds and their attached linters still remain to be processed. They, too, have many valuable uses.

 From Field to Mill

They are first moved from the cotton gins to cottonseed mills.

At a cottonseed mill the first step is to put the seeds through another kind of cotton gin. This cuts the longer linters away from the seeds, leaving the seeds with their shortest linters still attached. The longer linters that have been cut away at this stage are used to make such cotton products as mattresses, pillow stuffing, absorbent cotton, cord, and furniture stuffing.

In a final ginning step the remaining very short linters are cut away from their seeds. These shortest linters are made of almost pure cellulose (see p. 8), which is used to make such products as cellophane, rayon, and some plastics.

That leaves the seeds themselves. Some are kept whole for seeding later cotton crops. Most of the seeds, however, have other uses. First, they are cut open, separating their *hulls* (shells) from the *kernels* inside. The kernels contain *cottonseed oil*. This is pressed out of them and used in soap, cosmetics, shortening, several other oils, and a number of industrial products.

What is left of the kernels is used in such products as farm animal feed and several chemical products. Even the hulls are used, as animal feed and in various industrial products.

Even waste from cotton processing, like that being examined here, has value. It can be made into pellets for use as animal feed, fuel, or fertilizer.

For many centuries all the stages of turning cotton into thread were done by hand. This image from France in about 1470 shows a woman (right) spinning cotton by hand, while her servant (left) is carding (straightening and cleaning) more cotton for her to spin.

Cotton into Yarn

For thousands of years making cloth out of cotton has called for very similar kinds of skills and processes—whether for the simplest piece of clothing or the most complex and beautiful artwork.

Once separated from their seeds and cleaned (see p. 19), the longer cotton fibers (lint) are combed out and straightened so that the fibers run the same way. The fibers are then twisted so that they bind themselves together. Then they are spun into *yarn* on various kinds of *spindles* and *spinning wheels*. These came in many sizes and shapes, but all were designed to do the same thing: to twist the fibers into yarn of a relatively even width.

The yarn is often dyed in different colors. Then it is woven into cloth (see p. 27). Sometimes undyed yarn is woven into cloth and then later dyed. The resulting cloth can be of many colors, patterns, textures, and qualities, all depending on the threads and the kinds of weaves that were used.

22

Cotton into Yarn

Spinning and weaving have long been highly skilled crafts, practiced by individual spinners and weavers. That was certainly so earlier in human history, and it remains so in some parts of the world today.

Highly skilled spinners and weavers around the world still make many handmade cotton products using several kinds of spinning devices and weaving looms. Many of these are beautiful and unique works of art. (In earlier times many people also made their own dyes, but only a few do so now.) In the Guatemalan countryside, for example, some village women still grow and pick their own brown cotton, clean it, and take it through several other steps until they spin it into yarn. Then they weave it on their looms (see p. 27) into skirts, blouses, sashes, ribbons, and other kinds of cotton goods.

Machine-made Cloth

Yet by far the greatest amount of the world's cloth is today—and has been for hundreds of years—mass-produced by far less skilled people. They work at machines in the kinds

These are examples of some light brown and deeper brown cottons, along with a comb (right) used to straighten and clean the fibers and some traditional spindles (top left) used to spin fibers into yarn.

Cotton

Some cottons are of better quality than others. This man works as a cotton classer, grading cottons for certain kinds of uses in a Mississippi factory.

of highly mechanized cotton mills invented in Britain in the 1700s. Today the machines are different and much bigger, and they produce more and better cloth. Yet most of the basic processes have remained unchanged since cotton was first spun into yarn, woven into cloth, and made into clothing in ancient Mexico and India.

In a modern cotton mill the first step in creating cloth is to open the greatly compressed 500-pound bales of cotton. Workers usually combine cotton from several bales into a mass that is much looser and easier to clean. The cotton is then separated into small quantities and cleaned by strong jets of air.

After this cleaning the cotton is formed into thin sheets and passed through a *carding* machine. This somewhat straightens the twisted cotton fibers, cleans them further, and forms them into soft, ropelike strands called *slivers*.

 Cotton into Yarn

The slivers of cotton formed in carding are next drawn out into thinner slivers and twisted slightly to make them stronger. Often the cotton slivers are mixed or blended with different kinds of fibers to create combination substances, as when cotton and polyester slivers are put together and then spun into a cotton-polyester fabric used to make shirts. Whether mixed with other fibers or still all-cotton, the drawn-out slivers that result from this process are called *roving*.

The slivers of roving are likely to be drawn out even finer in further roving passes, until they are ready to be spun into yarn. Some long-staple cottons used to make expensive, high-quality products go

In modern factories cotton fibers are spun by machine onto large spools like this one. The spools are later used by other machines in weaving cotton cloth.

25

Cotton

through an additional cleaning and drawing-out process called *combing*.

Modern factory spinning is far faster than it was in earlier times. However, its basic principles are little changed. The most widely used system is *ring spinning*. In this process roving slivers are drawn out into their final thickness, given their final twist, and wound on a holder called a *bobbin*.

There are also several other spinning methods that are used less often. All are aimed at simplifying and speeding up the production of yarn. Some of them skip other steps in the yarn preparation process, including roving and twisting.

Many sports and exercise clothes are made of all cotton, like the sweatpants being worn here. Others are of cotton mixed with different threads, as in the stretchy top worn by this woman (front).

Pieces of cotton fabric were highly valued and saved for use in patchwork quilts. Some of these became works of art, like this one, the "Star of LeMoyne" quilt made in the United States between 1850 and 1875.

Yarn into Cloth

Weaving is a very old human skill. People were probably weaving baskets out of tree bark and other substances found in nature long before they began growing, spinning, and weaving cotton into cloth.

Weaving involves one set of threads (the *warp*) running lengthwise and the other set (the *filling* or *weft* threads) interlaced and running across the first, usually at right angles.

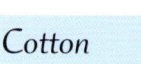 Cotton

In some parts of the world, yarn is still woven into cloth by hand, as these women are doing in Guatemala.

The basic tool used for weaving is a *loom*. It holds the warp yarns tight from end to end and sets the filling (weft) yarns across these, pushing the filling yarns into place. The result is cross-threaded cloth, as solid and strong as the yarns in it and the number of threads that meet and lock together to form the cloth.

Today there are more kinds of looms than there were thousands of years ago. Those looms are far faster and can do a good many more things than earlier looms. However, the kinds of weaves and cloth they create are basically the same as those made by skilled weavers using primitive looms in ancient times.

Several kinds of widely used weaves are commonly created on looms. The first and least expensive is the *plain weave*. It is also by far the most used of the world's weaves.

In plain weave the warp and filling yarns are simply interlaced at right angles to each other. The resulting cloth is suitable for making a very wide range of clothing and other woven goods. Plain weaves can be done in cotton. They can also be done using many other natural yarns (such as those made

Yarn into Cloth

of wool, silk, and linen) and also in many synthetic materials.

Cotton is also widely used in two other kinds of basic weaves. One of them is the very sturdy weave called *twill*. This weave has a pattern of diagonal (slanting) ribs. Three very well known cotton twills are denim, chino (which can also be made of wool), and cotton serge.

The third basic weave is cotton satin, called *sateen*, which has a smooth, glossy finish. This weave is used to make many kinds of clothing, as well as bedding and furniture coverings.

Cotton fabrics woven on large factory looms often have a very tight weave, so they are strong and long-lasting. That's why they are favored for so many uses, even in undyed white, as in the jacket worn by this boater.

This photograph of a cotton shirt collar, magnified 72 times, shows how the cotton threads are interwoven to form fabric. It also shows the many small tendrils of cotton that, over time, come loose and cause the fabric to fray.

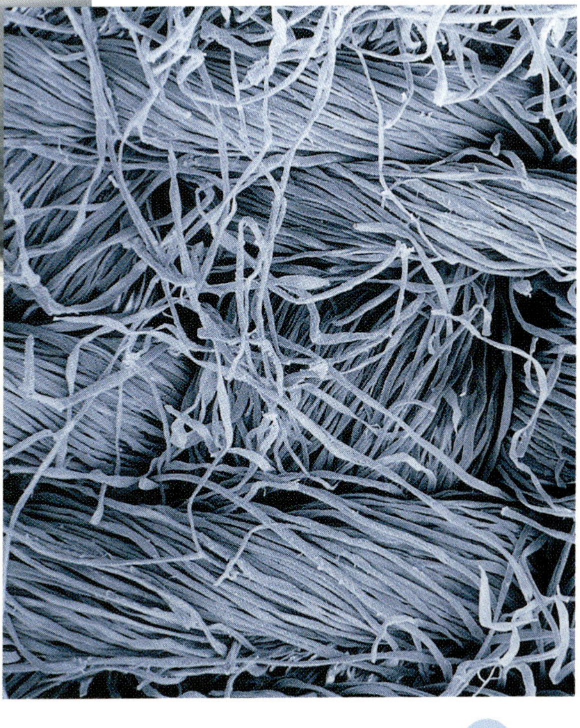

29

Cotton

Words to Know

bale Any large, tied bundle of material. Cotton bales contain roughly 500 pounds of cotton.

boll The seed pod at the center of a cotton flower, in which the cotton grows. When the boll bursts, the cotton is ready to be picked.

carbohydrate: See CELLULOSE.

carding In making YARN, a process that further cleans the cotton, passing it through a carding machine to straighten, clean, and form the cotton into SLIVERS.

cellulose A substance made of *glucose*; the major part of all plant fibers and tissues. Glucose is a *carbohydrate*, a kind of chemical compound that is composed of carbon, hydrogen, and oxygen.

combing In yarn-making, a step beyond CARDING, which further cleans and draws out (thins) some very high quality LONG-STAPLE COTTONS, making them ready to become SLIVERS of ROVING.

cotton gin A machine to separate cotton fibers from seeds, developed by Eli Whitney in 1793.

cottonseed oil An oil pressed out of the kernels (centers) of cottonseeds. It is used in several cotton by-products.

fiber Any natural or synthetic (humanmade) threadlike substance, such as cotton, that can be spun or otherwise formed into YARN.

filling: See WEFT.

fuzz: See LINTER.

glucose: See CELLULOSE.

hull The shell of the cottonseed.

kernel The inner portion (center) of the cottonseed.

lint The main body of the cotton FIBERS harvested from the cotton plant. Lint ranges from $\frac{1}{2}$ inch to 2 inches long.

linter The short cotton FIBERS ($\frac{1}{8}$ to $\frac{1}{2}$ inch long) left growing out of the cottonseed after the LINT fibers have been removed by the COTTON GIN. A second ginning process separates the linters from the cottonseed. Linter is also called *fuzz*.

long-staple cotton Cotton composed of FIBERS that are at least $1\frac{1}{8}$ inches long.

loom The basic tool used in WEAVING, which holds the WARP and WEFT threads in place as they are cross-threaded.

medium-staple cotton Cotton composed of FIBERS that are $1\frac{1}{32}$ to $1\frac{3}{32}$ inches long.

plain weave The most used of the world's basic weaves, in which the WARP and WEFT (filling) YARNS are interlaced at right angles to each other.

roving Cotton SLIVERS that have been made completely ready for the creation of YARN.

sateen weave A basic weave, which creates the smooth, glossy cotton fabric called *sateen*, with the look and feel of satin.

short-staple cotton Cotton composed of FIBERS that are up to an inch long.

sliver A group of cotton FIBERS somewhat twisted together, which form a longer strand of cotton that after processing can be spun into YARN.

spinning Making YARN out of FIBERS, using some kind of spinning machine, such as a *spinning wheel* or one of the kinds of very fast spinning devices used in modern cotton mills.

spinning wheel: See SPINNING.

trash: See WASTE.

twill weave A basic weave, which creates the sturdy cotton fabric called twill, used to make denim and several other kinds of clothing.

warp threads The lengthwise threads held in place by a LOOM.

waste Leaves, twigs, loose earth, and other materials picked up while harvesting cotton, which is removed before running the cotton through the cotton gin. Also called *trash*.

weaving The process of making cloth out of yarn on a loom.

weft The crosswise threads held in place by a loom, interlaced with the warp threads. Also called *filling*.

yarn The kind of long thread made out of cotton or other fibers, which is used to weave (see WEAVING), knit, or otherwise form fabrics.

On the Internet

The Internet has many interesting sites about cotton. The site addresses often change, so the best way to find current addresses is to go to a search site, such as www.yahoo.com. Type in a word or phrase, such as "cotton."

As this book was being written, websites about cotton included:

http://www.fabrics.net/cotton.asp
A section of Fabrics.Net focusing on cotton, with information about different kinds of cotton and fabrics woven from it.

http://msa.ars.usda.gov/ms/stoneville/uscgl/
Cotton Ginning Research Unit Homepage of the U.S. Agricultural Research Service, offering an overview of the modern ginning process, with images of the various machines used.

http://www.cottoninc.com/
Cotton Incorporated, including online articles about cotton and its use, care, and research, plus an explanation of terms.

http://www.interlog.com/~gwhite/ttt/tttintro.html
Textiles Through Time, a private website of links relating to textiles.

http://char.txa.cornell.edu/
Art, Design, and Visual Thinking, a site from Cornell University offering information about fibers, yarns, and design using them.

In Print

Your local library system will have various books on cotton. The following is just a sampling of them.

Burnham, Dorothy K. *Warp and Weft*. Toronto: Royal Ontario Museum, 1980.

Burton, Anthony. *The Rise and Fall of King Cotton*. London: British Broadcasting Company, 1984.

Corbman, Bernard P. *Textiles: Fiber to Fabric*. New York: McGraw-Hill, 1983.

Hammond, Winifred. *Cotton: From Farm to Market*. New York: Coward-McCann, 1968.

Kadolph, Sara J., and Anna L. Langford. *Textiles*. Upper Saddle River, NJ: Prentice-Hall, 1998.

Selsam, Millicent. *Cotton*. New York: Morrow, 1982.

Textiles: 5,000 Years. Jennifer Harris, ed. New York: Harry N. Abrams, 1993.

Van Nostrand's Scientific Encyclopedia, 8th ed., 2 vols. Douglas M. Considine and Glenn D. Considine, eds. New York: Van Nostrand Reinhold, 1995.

Wingate, Isabel B. *Textile Fibers and Their Selection*. Englewood Cliffs, NJ: Prentice-Hall, 1976.

Cotton

Index

Alabama 13
American cottons 9–10
Americas 5, 14
animal feed 21
Arizona 13
Arkansas 13
artificial fibers 11, 25, 29
artworks 15, 22–23, 27
Asia 10
Asiatic cottons 10
Assyria 15

Babylonia 15
bales, cotton 20, 24, 30
Bali 14
batik 14
Benin 16
bobbin 26
boll, cotton 6, 8–9, 30
boll weevil 8–9
Brazil 12–13
Britain 13, 16–18, 24

California 13
canvas 11, 13
carbohydrates 8. 30
carbon 8, 30
carding 22, 24–25, 30
carpets 11
cellophane 21
cellulose 7–8, 21, 30
China 5, 12–13
chino 29
Civil War 17–18
cleaning 19–20, 22–25, 30
climate 12–13
cloth 4–6, 11, 14–17, 20, 22–25, 27–29
clothing 4–5, 10, 14–15, 22–23, 25–26, 29
colored cotton 7
combing 26, 30
compounds 8
cosmetics 21
cotton gin 16–21, 30
cottonseed oil 4, 21, 30
cottonseeds 4, 6, 10, 16–17, 19–22, 30

Dahomey 16
denim 29
draperies 11
dyeing 7, 11, 14, 22–23

Ecuador 13, 15
Egypt 5, 7, 10, 12–13, 15
elements 8
Europe 17

factories 16–17, 20–21, 24–26, 28–29
fertilizer 21
fibers 6, 8–9, 11, 17, 19–25, 30
filling 27–28, 30
flower 6, 8, 30
France 22
fuel 21
fuzz: See **linter**

Georgia 13
ginning cotton 10, 16
Giza cotton 7
glucose 8, 30
Gossypium 8
Greece 13, 15
growing cotton 5, 8–9, 12
growing season 12
Guatemala 13, 15, 23, 28

harvesting 5, 8, 12, 18–19
hulls 21, 30
hydrogen 8, 30

India 5, 12–13, 15, 24
Indonesia 14
Indus Valley 15

kernels 21, 30

linen 29
lint 8–9, 19–20, 22, 30
linters 10, 19–21, 30
long-staple cotton 9, 15, 30
looms 23, 28–30

machines 5, 11, 16–17, 19–21, 23–26, 28–30
mass production 16–17
Mediterranean 15
medium-staple cotton 9, 30
Mexico 5, 12–13, 15, 24
Middle Ages 16
Middle East 15
mildew 11
mills: See **factories**
Mississippi 13, 24
mixed fabrics 4, 25–26

Native Americans 15
North, American 18

Old World 5
oxygen 8, 30

painting 11
Pakistan 12–13
Panama 7
Peru 5, 12–13, 15
picking cotton 5, 8, 12, 18–19, 23, 30
Pima cotton 7, 10
plain weave 28–30
plantation system 18
plastics 21
polyester 25
population 5
printing 11
processing cotton 5, 16–26

qualities of cotton 10–11
quilting 27

rayon 21
reaping 5
Renaissance 16
ring spinning 26
Rome 13, 15
roving 25, 30
Russia 12–13

sateen 29–30
satin 29–30
Sea Island cotton 10
seed: See **cottonseeds**

seed pod 6, 8, 30
serge 29
short-staple cotton 9, 30
shortening 4, 21
silk 1, 29
slavery 17–18
slivers 6, 24–25, 30
soap 21
South, American 17–18
spindles 22–23
spinning 4–6, 22–23, 25–27, 30
spinning wheel 22, 30
sugars 8
sunlight 11
synthetic fabrics 5, 25, 29–30

temperature 11–12
Tennessee 13
Texas 13
threads: See **yarns**
trash 19–21, 30
treating cotton 11
Turkey 13–14
twill 29–30

United States 5, 12–13, 16–18, 27
upholstery 4
Upland, American 9

varieties of cotton 7–10

warp 27–28, 30
waste 19–21, 30
water 7, 10, 12
wax 14
weaving 5, 13, 22–24, 27–30
weft 27–28, 30
West Africa 12, 16
Whitney, Eli 17, 30
wild cotton 8
wool 11, 29

yarns 5–7, 10–11, 15, 22–30

RECEIVED DEC 2 8 2004

$88: 269^{00}$ per set